Ride Without Fear

Confidence and Mindset Training for Anxious Equestrians

Mindful Rein Studio

Contents

For the Riders Who Sit in the Saddle and Still Feel Afraid ... v

Part 1
Understanding Your Fear

1. What Anxiety Looks Like in the Saddle ... 3
2. The Rider Brain ... 7
3. The Horse's Emotional Mirror ... 10

Part 2
Tools That Build Mental Strength

4. Breathing and Body Reset Techniques ... 15
5. The Confidence Toolkit ... 18
6. Riding with Curiosity Instead of Fear ... 22

Part 3
Returning After Scares or Setbacks

7. Fall and Trauma Recovery ... 27
8. Returning Adult Riders and Confidence Crises ... 30
9. Riding Through Physical Symptoms of Fear ... 33

Part 4
Working with Horses and Trainers

10. When Fear Comes from the Horse ... 39
11. Red and Green Flags in Coaching ... 43
12. Building a Partnership That Supports Confidence ... 46

Part 5
Goal Setting and Performing Under Pressure

13. Mindset Training for Shows and Clinics — 51
14. Realistic Goal Setting for Nervous Riders — 57
15. The Confident Rider Lifestyle — 60

Part 6
Practical Workbooks

16. Rider Training Worksheets — 65

Afterword: Confidence Is a Skill You Build, Not a Personality Trait — 75
The Voice Behind this Book — 79

For the Riders Who Sit in the Saddle and Still Feel Afraid

If you are holding this book, there is a good chance you love horses more than anything, but when riding, part of you feels tight in the chest. You may feel it when your horse takes a bigger stride than expected. Or when someone asks you to canter. Or the moment you enter a show ring and your heartbeat becomes louder than your trainer's voice.

Maybe you can ride well. You understand the theory. You know how to sit tall and how to use your aids. You know what you are supposed to do, but yet, your body reacts as if danger is everywhere...

You are not weak or a bad rider...and you are not alone!

Anxiety shows up quietly in stables all over the world. Riders who were once confident suddenly freeze after a fall. New riders worry that every mistake will end badly and adults who return to riding carry pressure, responsibility, and fear of getting hurt again.

For the Riders Who Sit in the Saddle and Still Feel Afraid

Rather see fear as your friend - your mind is simply trying to protect you. Fear is a safety system, your brain asking a question. It is not an enemy to fight but a message to understand.

This book is not about forcing bravery or about comparing yourself to riders who seem fearless. True confidence is not loud, it does not rush, and does not ignore fear. Confidence is built slowly, the same way trust is built with a horse.

Here, we will explore how your brain learns fear and how it can learn courage. You will discover breathing tools that quiet your mind, and routines that reset tension. We will also discuss techniques that help you ride with clarity even when you feel nervous. You will learn how to reshape your thoughts, and how to communicate with your horse during anxious moments,. This will create a partnership where both of you feel supported.

Your riding journey does not need to be a battle - you will learn a way forward that respects your feelings and strengthens your confidence without pressure.

Let this be the moment you decide that fear is not the end of your story. It is simply a chapter.

A part of the process and a signal that you are ready to learn something new.

Turn the page. Your courage is waiting to be trained.

    Annalie
    Founder of Mindful Rein Studio, Horsewoman, and educator with decades in the saddle.

Part 1
Understanding Your Fear

Chapter 1
What Anxiety Looks Like in the Saddle

Fear in riding does not always show itself in dramatic ways. It is not only the rider who trembles before a jump or bursts into tears. Sometimes fear is quiet. It looks like waiting a little longer before asking for canter, or telling yourself you will try that new exercise next week. Many riders learn to stay safe by choosing familiar horses, sticking to simple routines, and pretending their nerves do not exist. Over time those choices begin to feel normal, and the rider forgets how much worry shapes every decision in the saddle.

Subtle Signs Riders Often Miss

Most people notice fear only when it becomes overwhelming. A shaky breath, a sudden stop in front of a fence, or hands that yank the reins are easy to spot. The first signs arrive long before that point, and they appear gently, almost unnoticed. For example:

The rider is gripping with the knees without meaning to,

leaning forward as if something might go wrong, or even pulling on the reins even while trying to soften

These are not bad habits. They are natural reactions your body uses to protect you. Even when you want to ride with freedom and balance, your nervous system tries to shield you from anything it considers risky.

> *When I was a child, I rode a pony named Molly who taught me more about nerves than any trainer did. She was steady and kind, but the moment I tightened my hands, she would lift her head and rush forward as if she sensed trouble. I did not understand at the time that I was holding my breath. The day a quiet instructor asked me to exhale at every corner, Molly settled instantly. I learned that even a safe pony reacts to the tension we carry.*

Why the Body Reacts With Tension

When your brain senses a threat, it prepares your body to survive. It does not understand the difference between a young horse spooking at a shadow and a genuine danger from the wild. Its reaction is automatic. Shaking comes from adrenaline that prepares muscles for action. Stiff hands come from the upper body tightening. Tight knees happen because the brain wants to protect your trunk. Holding your breath is part of a freeze response

These reactions are not signs of poor riding ability. They are biological instincts that can be reshaped with awareness and training.

The Fight or Flight Response in the Saddle

Humans stay alive by reacting quickly. That survival instinct shows up when a horse speeds up or hesitates. The brain tells the body to respond instantly with movement that feels protective, such as:

Freezing in the saddle, clamping onto the horse for stability, pulling backward to feel in control, leaning forward to brace for a fall. or scanning the surroundings quickly

These reactions once helped us survive real danger, but they interfere with clear communication between horse and rider. They make timing, balance, and softness difficult.

How Fear Affects the Horse

Horses feel changes in a rider's body before the rider notices them. They respond not to words, but to posture, breath, and tension.

Gripping tells the horse to tense or move faster, tight hands blur the clarity of rein aids. Leaning forward encourages the horse to rush and a stiff jaw or back invites the horse to tighten in return

The horse is not misbehaving. It is responding to the rider's body in the same way the rider is responding to fear. The tension moves between both partners until it feels like the horse created the problem, when in truth both are reacting to each other in a cycle.

Understanding this shared feedback is the key to breaking it. You cannot find real confidence by ignoring fear or trying to overpower it. Confidence comes from helping both your mind and body feel safe, so that your horse can feel safe with you.

Chapter 2
The Rider Brain

The Rider Brain

Many riders get frustrated with themselves when they feel scared. They think they should be braver, or that talented riders do not struggle with fear. They try to push it away or hide it. But fear is not a sign of weakness. It is simply the brain doing its job.

How Your Brain Responds to Speed, Height, and Surprises

The brain is designed to protect you. Movement is one of the things that triggers this protective system. Horses move quickly, they shift their weight without warning, and they react before we have time to think. Your brain pays attention to that.

You might want to canter, but your brain may not feel ready. The jump might be tiny, yet your brain may focus on what could go wrong. Your horse might be calm, but your brain notices that it is still stronger than you.

The brain responds to what it senses, not to your logic. It reacts first and thinks later. When you understand this, you stop blaming yourself for being afraid.

The Survival Loop and Why Thinking Becomes Hard

Once fear is activated, the brain starts a protection cycle:

- It looks for possible danger
- It tenses the body to prepare for a fall or sudden movement
- It interprets that tension as more proof of danger
- It increases fear to try to keep you safe

This is why fear can grow even when your horse is doing nothing wrong. Your body tightens, and the brain reads that tension as a sign of threat. The cycle continues until you interrupt it by calming the body.

> *While retraining an off-track Thoroughbred named Jasper, I felt my heart race every time his stride lengthened. He was not misbehaving. He was just used to moving forward with power, and my body still remembered past falls with other horses. When I paused, breathed, and asked again only when my shoulders felt soft, his transitions changed. I was not training him. I was teaching my nervous system that the same moment could be safe again.*

Why One Scary Ride Stays in Your Memory

The brain remembers fear more strongly than success because it wants to keep you alive. One fall, or even one unexpected bolt or buck, can leave a lasting memory. It is not punishment. It is learning.

This is why you might forget hundreds of great rides but remember one frightening one very clearly. You are not stuck in the past. Your brain is protecting your future.

Training the Brain to Learn Confidence

The brain can learn bravery the same way it learned fear. Not through pressure, and not by forcing yourself to be bold, but through small experiences of success. The goal is not to get rid of fear. The goal is to help the brain realize that you can be safe and confident at the same time.

You can train your brain like you train a young horse: Start with small steps, make sure you use clear signals, be consistent, never punish fear and always reward calm progress

Every quiet moment in the saddle teaches your brain that it can relax. Every simple exercise that you handle well builds real confidence. Courage grows from feeling safe enough to stay curious, not from trying to pretend fear does not exist.

Chapter 3
The Horse's Emotional Mirror

Horses are incredibly aware of the emotions behind our actions. Long before we pick up the reins or ask for a trot, they already know how we feel. They pay attention to body language in a way most people never notice. The breath we take, the way we sit, even where we look tells them more than our words or aids.

How Horses Notice Tension

Horses pick up on things such as:

- The rhythm and depth of the riders breathing

- How tight or soft our muscles are, especially in the legs and seat

- Where our eyes move and how focused we are

- How quickly we react

- The overall energy in our posture

Horses do not understand fear as an idea. They feel fear through the body that carries them. A tight rider makes a horse prepare for something to go wrong. A soft rider allows the horse to let go.

Why Nervous Riders Create Nervous Horses

When a rider gets tense, the horse reads it as a warning. The horse does not know that the nervousness might be about riding itself. It simply assumes that something around it is unsafe. The horse is not the cause of the nerves. It is reacting to what the rider's body is saying.

This is why calm riders often do well with anxious horses. A steady body communicates safety far better than confidence in words.

How to Break the Tension Cycle

The spiral of tension usually looks like this:

Rider becomes anxious - horse feels the anxiety and becomes alert or reactive - the rider becomes more afraid and both become even more tense.

To stop this pattern, you do not need to force yourself to relax. You only need to release small physical signs of tension.

Try interrupting the cycle by: softening the breath, exhale for longer, allowing the thigh muscles to loosen, opening the chest gently without lifting the shoulders, and letting your weight sink naturally into the saddle.

These signals tell the horse that everything is safe. The horse responds with calmness, and the rider begins to feel safer because of the horse. A new partnership starts.

The Quiet Core Technique

The Quiet Core is an easy reset for riders who feel nervous.

Step 1: Exhale through the mouth until the air feels empty

Step 2: Let the lower ribs soften as you inhale again

Step 3: Allow the seat to feel heavy on the saddle, not tight

Step 4: Let the arms move with the horse instead of resisting the movement

Step 5: Focus on rhythm rather than control

The aim is not strength. The aim is softness with intention. Horses look for relaxation the same way we look for reassurance. When you offer it, they trust you.

Part 2
Tools That Build Mental Strength

Chapter 4
Breathing and Body Reset Techniques

Calm riding begins in your body long before it shows in your seat or your hands. The way you breathe sends messages to your nervous system, your posture, and even to your horse. Many people think fear starts in the mind, but most of the time it begins with short, shallow breaths that make the body feel unsafe. When your breath slows down, the rest of your body loosens as well, and your horse senses that change immediately.

Box Breathing

This is one of the simplest and most helpful techniques for riders because it quiets the mind and steadies the hands. The pattern is easy to remember.

Inhale for four counts - Hold for four counts - Exhale for four counts - Hold for four counts - Repeat.

The idea is not to take bigger breaths, but to teach your body to stay steady. It works before getting on, during stressful moments, and after something frightening happens. It clears the mind and helps you respond, rather than react.

Breathing with the Gait

Every gait has a rhythm. When you breathe with that rhythm instead of fighting it, both you and your horse feel more settled.

Walk - Breathe in for two steps, then breathe out for two

Trot - Inhale for one diagonal pair, exhale for the next

Canter - Inhale for one stride, exhale for two

These patterns give you something predictable to focus on, which keeps you from overthinking. Your attention goes to the movement, not the fear.

The Calm Half Halt

A half halt is not only a riding aid. It can also be a reset for your mind. A calm half halt uses breath and balance to steady the horse without tightening the body.

Start with a slow exhale and soften the ribs. Close your fingers lightly without gripping and your seat deepen. Then release into the movement again

This quiet moment helps the horse rebalance and helps your body stay clear and precise rather than tense or hurried.

Grounding Breath During a Spook

When a horse jumps or startles, many riders react by gasping and tightening their muscles. A grounding breath interrupts that instinct.

Exhale fully through the mouth - Let your shoulders drop - Sink your weight into both stirrups - Keep the reins soft instead of pulling

This tells the horse there is nothing to fear. A calm rider during a spook teaches the horse to recover more quickly.

How to Practice, On and Off the Horse

These habits become natural when you train them regularly.

Unmounted practice

Use box breathing twice a day.

Place a hand on your abdomen to feel the breath move.

Walk and match your breathing to your steps.

Mounted practice

Start each ride with three rounds of box breathing.

Use rhythm breathing during transitions.

Take a grounding breath whenever you feel tension rising.

Your breath is your first tool for safety, clarity, and confidence. It is not just a technique, it is the foundation of a calm and capable rider.

Chapter 5
The Confidence Toolkit

Confidence is not a mystery or a gift some people are simply born with. It grows from habits and tools that help you through the moments that feel difficult. When you have a plan, your mind settles and stops sending out urgent alarms. Think of the ideas below as a rider's toolkit for staying grounded.

Creating a Personal Mantra

A mantra is a short phrase that captures the rider you want to become. It should feel honest, easy to remember, and supportive. A few examples are:

> I ride with calm intention.
> My breath leads my body.
> I choose steady progress.
> My horse feels safe with me.

Say your mantra when you mount, during transitions, or when doubt starts to creep in. It becomes something steady to hold on to.

> *A beginner rider I taught years ago whispered the same phrase before every transition on a nervous Thoroughbred we were retraining. Her mantra was simple. "Steady seat." She said it quietly and repeated it before every aid. By the end of the ride, the horse moved with balance and ease. She did not build confidence by being brave. She built it by giving her mind something calm to follow.*

Emergency Reset Plan

Fear grows quickly when you feel you have lost control. An emergency reset plan gives you something simple to follow when your thoughts start to race.

Stop - Exhale Press your heels down - Walk a small circle - Reassess without pressure.

These steps interrupt fear and bring your focus back to the present moment.

Fear Ladder Training

A fear ladder takes a big challenge and breaks it into small wins. This keeps your brain from feeling overwhelmed. For example, if cantering makes you nervous:

Canter for a single stride - Canter half the arena - Canter one full lap - Add a transition inside the gait - Canter a simple pattern.

You build confidence one step at a time, and each step teaches your mind that success is possible.

Confidence Cards for the Grooming Box

These are small cards you can keep with your brushes or tack. Before you ride, choose one to guide your mindset. Each card can hold a reminder, a breathing cue, or a calming thought. For example:

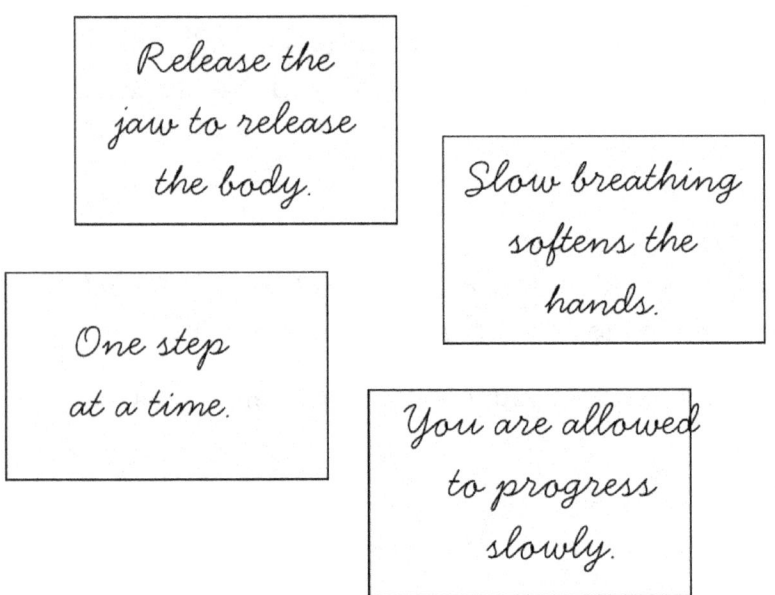

These cards feel helpful because they support you in the exact moment you need it.

Five Minute Pre Ride Mental Warm Up

We often remember to stretch our muscles but forget to prepare our mind. A short mental warm up can change the way your whole ride feels.

- Minute one: Slow, deep breathing.

- Minute two: Repeat your mantra.

- Minute three: Visualise a calm, successful ride.

- Minute four: Stretch your shoulders and hips.

- Minute five: Choose one clear goal.

When your mind arrives prepared, your body follows with more ease.

Chapter 6
Riding with Curiosity Instead of Fear

Fear often tries to keep you safe by imagining the worst outcome. Curiosity does something very different. It shifts your attention from danger to discovery, and it gives your mind a job that actually helps you. Riders who stay curious tend to stay present, solve problems with a calmer mindset, and keep their thoughts from spiralling.

How Curiosity Changes Fear

Fear tells your brain that something bad is coming. Curiosity encourages you to notice what is actually happening in this moment. The two cannot exist fully at the same time. When curiosity grows stronger, fear naturally fades.

Curiosity leads you to ask simple questions such as

- What did my horse react to

- What part of my body feels tight

- What small adjustment can I make right now

With these questions, your brain becomes a helpful partner instead of a threat detector.

Switching from Judgment to Observation

Many riders judge themselves harshly, and judgment fuels more fear. Observation, on the other hand, brings understanding and clarity.

Judgment sounds like:

> I always mess this up
> I am not good enough
> Everyone is watching me

Observation sounds like

> My shoulders are tight
> My horse lost rhythm
> I need a lighter hand

Observation gives you useful information that helps you improve, without attacking yourself in the process.

Focusing on What Is Working

Fear looks for problems. Curiosity notices what is stable and going well. In every ride there is at least one thing that is working. When you acknowledge it, confidence grows.

For example

> My hands are steady today
> My horse is responding to my leg
> The rhythm is getting better

You are not ignoring challenges. You are grounding yourself in what is already working so you can build from there.

A Simple Way to Reframe Mistakes

To anxious riders, mistakes often feel dangerous, yet they are simply part of learning. Reframing them helps your brain stay calm and focused.

Try this process

- Step one: Notice the mistake without reacting to it

- Step two: Identify the cause

- Step three: Choose one small correction

- Step four: Move on right away

This keeps your mind from spiralling and turns every mistake into a learning moment.

Part 3
Returning After Scares or Setbacks

Chapter 7
Fall and Trauma Recovery

A fall usually brings more than bruises or soreness. Even after the physical pain has faded, the nervous system holds on to the experience. Riders often think they should just get back on and push through the fear, but the brain does not respond to pressure. It responds to feeling safe.

What Your Body Really Remembers

The brain keeps a sharp record of frightening moments. This is not a flaw, it is a survival skill. After a fall, your nervous system may hold on to details such as:

- The pace just before the accident
- The angle of the horse's movement
- The sensation of being unable to react
- The last thing you saw or heard
- The instant you lost balance

When your body recognises similar movement or speed, it tries to protect you, even if you are actually safe. You are not being dramatic. Your brain is trying to stop you from getting hurt again.

A Safe and Steady Way Back to the Saddle

Returning to riding works best when done step by step. Each stage allows your brain to experience success and safety.

Start with grooming and slow breathing beside your horse. Mount, sit quietly for a moment, then dismount with calm breath control. Walk without goals, paying attention to how your body feels. Add slow circles or simple patterns that feel predictable. Try trot or canter only when the walk feels completely secure

There is no benefit in rushing. The aim is to feel safe during each step, not to move faster.

How Slow Exposure Helps Riders Heal

Slow exposure teaches the brain to respond calmly again. This involves repeating small actions until they feel ordinary. For example, if canter transitions scare you, do not start with a full canter session. You can begin with:

One stride of canter - Return to trot - Breathe - Repeat gently

The goal is not speed or distance. The goal is to build trust in your ability to stop or adjust whenever you need to.

How Trust Grows After a Fall

Trust does not grow by pretending fear is not there. Trust grows when you choose actions that make your body feel protected. You can build confidence by:

- Riding a steady, calm horse before returning to a more challenging one
- Working with a trainer who understands fear
- Riding in a quiet space before attempting busy arenas
- Staying within your comfort zone until calm becomes natural

Trust develops when your nervous system no longer feels under threat.

Knowing When to Reach Out for Support

Many riders try to handle fear alone and end up struggling more. Reaching out for guidance is a skill. It shows strength, not weakness. Helpful support may include a trainer who works with nervous riders, physiotherapist to address pain or tension,Counselling to work through trauma, lessons on a reliable schoolmaster to restore confidence and a medical review if symptoms do not improve

Healing is not about being tough. It is about finding the right tools, creating safety, and allowing progress at a pace that supports both body and mind.

Chapter 8
Returning Adult Riders and Confidence Crises

Many adults come back to riding after a long break. What they believe they can still do often feels very different once they are back in the saddle. The mind remembers clearly. The body needs time to catch up. It is easy to feel confident in theory, yet overwhelmed by the reality of riding again. That gap can bring frustration and second guesses.

Anxiety After Time Away

Stepping away from horses for years changes how people look at risk. Adults tend to carry more awareness. They think about injuries, bills, recovery time, and how life would be affected if something went wrong. The brain grows careful with age, not because we are weaker, but because we understand how valuable our bodies are.

Balancing Responsibilities and Risk

Many adult riders feel guilty for being nervous. They do not want to disappoint their horse, their instructor, or the people at the barn. They worry about being judged. It can help to remember that riding is a choice made for personal wellbeing, not a test to pass.

Ask yourself:

- What does riding give me?

- What level of risk feels reasonable?

- What pace feels right for my current abilities?

Riding does not need to be intense to be meaningful.

Confidence, Stamina, and Strength

It is easy to mistake physical limitations for fear. A tight or shaky body does not always mean anxiety. Sometimes it is simply a sign of reduced strength or balance. Think of these as three separate tools you are rebuilding:

- Confidence: believing in your skills

- Stamina: keeping your body moving comfortably

- Strength: staying stable in the saddle

If your legs tremble, it may be muscle fatigue, not panic. If your hands feel unsteady, the issue could be posture rather than fear. Better fitness supports confidence because your body becomes more reliable.

> *I once worked with a returning adult rider who had excellent instincts from childhood but could not understand why his legs shook after ten minutes of trot. He assumed it was fear. After a few weeks of gentle fitness work, the shaking disappeared and his confidence*

grew. He had not been scared at all. His body simply needed support to match the expectations in his mind.

Support Without Pressure

Adult riders do best when they feel supported instead of rushed. Accountability should inspire progress without stress. This can come from a patient instructor, a friend who rides at the same level, journal keeping for tracking small wins, and monthly check ins that focus on growth, not mistakes

Accountability encourages effort. Pressure demands perfection.

Creating a Progress Map

A personal progress map brings clarity. Divide your skills into three groups:

Comfort zone: things you can do calmly

Stretch zone: things that challenge you a little

Outside your limit: things you are not ready for yet

Spend most of your practice moving gently between the first two. Write down your progress each week. You will see steady improvement on paper, even when it feels slow in the moment.

Chapter 9
Riding Through Physical Symptoms of Fear

Fear often shows up as physical sensations long before the rider realises it. The body gives signals that the brain is preparing for danger. Learning to respond calmly to symptoms keeps fear from escalating.

Racing Heartbeat

A fast heart rate does not mean danger. It means preparation. To regain control:

- Breathe out longer than you breathe in
- Focus your eyes on a fixed point for three seconds
- Feel the weight of your seat in the saddle

These steps teach your heart that the body is safe.

Shaky Arms

Shaking hands or arms are often caused by adrenaline and gripping. To reduce it:

- Release the elbows
- Breathe while counting three strides
- Imagine your hands floating rather than holding

Softness weakens the fear response.

Numb Legs or Tense Grip

Numbness happens when the nervous system constricts muscles. To reset:

- Drop your thigh weight
- Let the lower leg hang heavy
- Rebalance from seat instead of gripping

Tension decreases when the legs release control.

Sweaty Hands

Sweaty hands are an early sign of adrenaline. Instead of judging it, use it as a reminder to reset.

- Rub reins gently between fingers
- Loosen grip without letting reins slip
- Focus on smooth breathing rather than drying hands

This turns a symptom into a cue for calmness.

A Physical Calm Down Routine

Use this anytime tension rises during a ride.

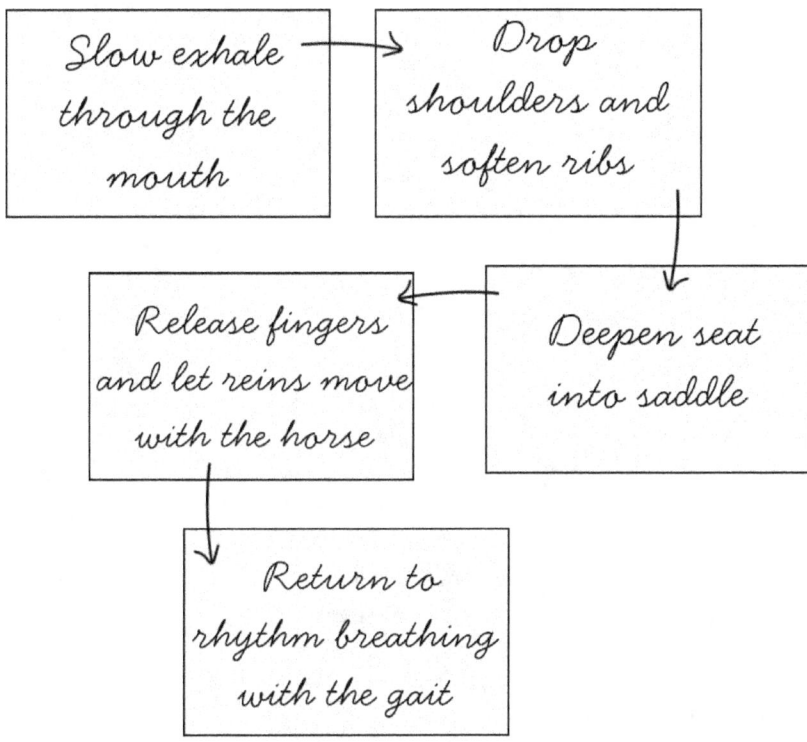

Repeat until breath and movement feel connected again.

Physical reactions are not signs of weakness. They are messages. Instead of fighting them, guide them. When your body learns safety, your mind follows.

Part 4

Working with Horses and Trainers

Chapter 10
When Fear Comes from the Horse

Fear does not only come from what goes on in the rider's head. Sometimes the way a horse reacts can make anyone feel unsure. Horses are never difficult on purpose. They respond to their environment, to how they were raised and trained, and to what your body is telling them. When you understand different types of horses, it becomes easier to choose a partner who supports your confidence.

Spooky Horses

A spooky horse notices everything. A sudden sound or a moving shadow might make it jump, even if nothing is truly dangerous. This can make riders feel nervous, even when the spooks are small.

Try these habits with spooky horses:

Keep your breath slow and deep and focus your eyes on where you are going, not on what scared them. Let the neck bend slightly so the body stays relaxed. Circle near the scary object to create rhythm and familiarity

> Never punish a spook, instead reward any sign of curiosity

Confidence with spooky horses comes from rhythm and softness, not force.

Fast Horses

Some horses naturally want to move forward. Pulling harder usually makes them push harder in return. Fighting speed only creates more speed.

Instead, try this:

Breathe out during half halts. Use your seat to slow the movement, not your hands. Let out a long exhale every few strides. Ride circles with your inside leg guiding direction rather than blocking speed

> Reward even the smallest slowing of pace

Fast horses settle when the rider relaxes instead of tightening.

Horses with Big Movement

A powerful trot or canter can feel overwhelming at first. The lift of the stride can make a rider feel unsteady or unsure.

To build trust with big movement:

Work in short intervals within each gait. Let your breath move with the horse, not against it. Focus on following the motion rather than controlling it. Think of your body as heavy and grounded, not stiff. Strengthen your seat gradually over time

Large movement becomes exciting rather than intimidating once your body flows with it.

Unpredictable Horses

Some horses change quickly from calm to tense. This may come from pain, fear, confusion, or inconsistent handling. If you do not feel safe, it is not your responsibility to fix the problem.

Signs you might need a different horse for confidence:

- Sudden bucking, spinning, or dramatic reactions

- Signs of pain or discomfort

- Even professionals struggle to keep the horse relaxed

You deserve a horse that supports your emotional safety as you learn.

> *As a young trainer, I worked with a beautiful, reactive warmblood who made even skilled riders tense. I tried for months to build trust with him, but the partnership never felt safe. When I switched my focus to a calm, thoughtful mare instead, both my training progress and my confidence grew. Some horses teach us that bravery begins with choosing the right partner, not proving we can handle the hardest one.*

Matching Rider Personality to Horse Type

Horses have personalities and so do riders. A good match helps confidence grow without effort.

Think about your traits:

If you like predictability, choose a calm and steady horse

If you enjoy challenges, a sensitive horse may suit your style

f you love forward energy, a quick horse may feel fun rather than scary

If you need time to build trust, choose a horse that patiently allows slow progress

The best horse is not the boldest or the most impressive. The best horse is the one that makes you feel safe enough to grow, learn, and enjoy the ride.

Chapter 11
Red and Green Flags in Coaching

The right coach helps you grow as a rider. The wrong one can make you doubt yourself. You deserve lessons that feel encouraging, clear, and suited to your pace. No rider should walk into the arena feeling rushed or judged.

What a Supportive Instructor Looks Like

A good instructor creates a positive learning space and:

- Explains exercises in a way that makes sense

- Offers solutions instead of tearing you down

- Respects your pace and personal limits

- Focuses on progress rather than perfection

- Helps you develop skills that actually fit your horse

Learning should feel safe, structured, and realistic.

Language That Builds Confidence

The words a coach uses matter. They can lift your confidence or shut it down. Supportive teaching will guide you without shaming you, and they keep your mind open to learning.

How to Speak Up in Lessons

You are allowed to ask for what you need. Your instructor cannot read your mind. Clear communication keeps you safe and calm. Helpful phrases might be:

- I feel tense, can we slow this down

- I am not ready for that exercise yet

- Can we break this into smaller steps

- I need a moment to breathe and reset

Confidence grows when you advocate for yourself.

When It May Be Time to Change Trainers

You do not owe loyalty to a coach who damages your confidence. It might be time to move on if:

- You feel anxious before every lesson

- Mistakes are met with irritation instead of guidance

- Your boundaries are dismissed

- Riding starts to feel like a chore rather than something you love

If you decide to leave, you can do it with respect. A simple message works:

I appreciate what I have learned, but I need an instructor who supports my confidence goals at this time.

Ride Without Fear

Growth sometimes means choosing a new path, and that choice belongs to you.

Chapter 12
Building a Partnership That Supports Confidence

Confidence does not start the moment you sit in the saddle. It grows long before that, through simple habits and calm communication. You and your horse are two living bodies learning how to trust each other, step by step.

Building trust on the ground

Groundwork gives you a shared language without the pressure of riding. Try slow, thoughtful work that invites your horse to relax with you such as: Lead with an easy rhythm instead of rushing. Ask for a soft, relaxed backup from light cues. Gently flex the neck to each side without force. Walk circles while letting your breathing guide the pace. Use slow, steady touch to help desensitise

When a horse learns to trust your hands and body on the ground, that trust naturally follows into the saddle.

A calm start to every ride

A predictable beginning makes riding feel safe for both of you. Simple routines help your body settle and help your horse understand what to expect.

One example might be start with slow, mindful grooming. Stretch the neck with a treat to encourage relaxation. Walk together for a few minutes in hand. Mount quietly and take one deep breath together. Begin with soft walk circles before moving on.

Repeating this routine teaches your horse that nothing unpredictable is about to happen. It also reminds your own mind that there is no need to rush.

Creating shared expectations

Both horse and rider feel more confident when the goal is clear. Set expectations that feel realistic for the day.

> Today we focus only on soft transitions
> We will trot only if the walk feels relaxed
> We stop when the horse genuinely tries
> Calm effort matters more than perfection

Clear goals remove pressure and help both of you succeed.

Rewarding even the smallest progress

Growth shows up in tiny pieces. Confidence comes from noticing them.

- A lowered head

- A quiet, tension free halt

- One relaxed corner

- A balanced circle that feels easy

- A transition that does not rush

Celebrate these moments as soon as they happen. A warm voice, a gentle pat, or a short break can make a big difference. Horses repeat what feels rewarding. So do riders.

Part 5
Goal Setting and Performing Under Pressure

Chapter 13
Mindset Training for Shows and Clinics

Riders often think confidence comes from having a good day in the ring. In reality, it starts much earlier. It grows in the quiet moments, in your daily habits, and especially in how you prepare your mind. A show or clinic is not a pass or fail test of your talent. It is a chance to practise your focus in a new setting. You are not there to perform for other people. You are there to strengthen the way you think.

You cannot control how your horse feels at a new venue, how busy the warm up gets, or what other riders are doing. You can control your thoughts, your breathing, and what you expect from yourself. Pressure eases when you stop chasing perfection. Real progress starts when you ride to learn, not to impress.

The Pre-Show Mind Warm Up

Just like you warm up your horse's body, your mind needs a warm up too. If you skip it, your brain walks into a busy environment unprepared. It tries to keep you safe by tensing up and racing ahead. A calm mind does not magically appear when things feel high pressure. You train it on purpose.

Here is a simple five step pre-show mind warm up you can use every time.

One: Breathe before you leave the car

Take three slow breaths with long, gentle exhales. The goal is not "deep" breathing, it is slow breathing that tells your nervous system, "I am safe."

Two: Choose one goal only

Pick one small, clear riding goal for this ride. For example: Keep the same rhythm in every transition, soften the rein after each half halt or finish each jump with a soft hand.

Your goal should be simple enough that you can remember it when your nerves kick in.

Three: Walk the area slowly

Do not rush through the warm up spaces. Stroll around first. Feel the ground under your feet, notice the sounds and smells, and give your body time to adjust before you get on. This helps prevent sensory overload.

Four: Visualise one calm moment

Choose one moment from your ride, such as your first transition, first halt, or first trot circle. Picture it being relaxed, not perfect. You are training your brain to feel safe, not to chase a win.

Five: Repeat your mantra

Use a short phrase as your mental anchor. For example:

> My breath guides my ride
> Calm, then clear
> Rhythm first

Say it out loud or in your head before you tighten the girth or swing into the saddle.

This whole warm up tells your mind, "I am prepared, and I have a plan." You are going into the ring to apply that plan, not to prove your worth.

Visualisation That Actually Reduces Mistakes

Visualisation is not just daydreaming. When you picture yourself doing something, your body quietly practises it. Your nervous system responds as if you are already riding. The problem is that many riders visualise what they are afraid of. They replay refusals, rushing, missed leads, or forgotten courses in their heads. This teaches the brain to expect those problems.

To use visualisation in a helpful way:

Visualise small moments, not the whole round

Your mind works best with short, simple scenes. Try picturing things like a relaxed halt at the start, a smooth, even trot circle, calm exhale before the first jump, our seat deepening and following after landing, and a steady rhythm through the corner. See these in your minds eye, experience it as if it really happens.

These tiny calm moments give your brain something clear and achievable to create again.

Do not chase perfect rounds in your head

Perfection adds pressure. Instead of imagining a ride with zero mistakes, imagine how you calmly recover.

For example, picture making a steady correction after a deep distance. letting out a breath after an accidental trot step, resetting the rhythm after a spook or keeping your hand soft after a fast corner

You are training resilience, not flawless riding. The goal is to stay steady when things are messy, because real rides are always a little messy.

Confidence Cues in the Warm Up

Warm up arenas can feel like chaos. Horses are moving in every direction, riders are overtaking you, and it can seem as if everyone is watching. You cannot control that environment, but you can decide how you move through it.

Confidence cues are small, physical actions you use to steady yourself in the middle of that busyness.

Try using cues like these during warm up:

• Let your breath drop into your belly before every transition

• Allow your elbows to follow your horse's movement instead of locking them

• Count quietly under your breath, "one two, one two," to keep a steady rhythm

• Soften your face with a small smile to relax your jaw and neck

- Give your horse a gentle stroke on the neck after a simple effort

- Focus your eyes on the space you are riding into, not on the people around you

You are not there to impress the warm up arena. You are there to make your body a calm, safe place for your horse.

How to Handle Ring Errors in the Moment

Mistakes will always happen. Riders usually lose confidence not because something went wrong, but because of the way they respond to it. The brain's first reaction is often to panic, freeze, or try to fix everything all at once. Calm riding needs a clear, repeatable plan you can use even when you feel flustered.

Use this three step response whenever something goes wrong.

Step one: Exhale

Before you change anything, breathe out. Let your shoulders soften. A tight, snappy correction usually creates more problems.

Step two: Fix one thing only

Choose the single most useful adjustment. For example to fix rhythm before position, ix straightness before speed, or to fix balance before direction

One clear correction is far more effective than five rushed ones.

Step three: Continue with curiosity

Instead of criticising yourself or your horse, ask, "What does my horse need from me now?" Think like a problem solver, not a judge.

When you treat mistakes this way, they stop feeling dangerous. They turn into information you can use. Each error becomes one more chance to practise calm thinking, and that is where real confidence comes from.

Chapter 14
Realistic Goal Setting for Nervous Riders

Many riders set goals because they are watching what everyone else is doing. They try to jump higher, go faster, or compete at impressive shows simply because their friends are doing it. Nervous riders often need something different. Your goals should protect your emotional wellbeing and help you grow your bravery step by step. Real confidence comes from intention, not from chasing bigger achievements.

Goals That Strengthen You From Within

A meaningful riding goal should improve your mindset, not just your performance. Notice the difference:

Ego focused goals might sound like:

Jump ninety centimetres by spring. Place in the top three at the next show. Learn flying changes within a month.

Character building goals might sound like:

Keep breathing through transitions. Maintain a steady rhythm for the whole ride. Ride forward without gripping too tightly.

Goals like these create skills that naturally lead to better results.

Confidence is not the same as winning a ribbon. Confidence is being able to stay focused and effective in the moment.

Redefining Success Beyond Ribbons

A ribbon rewards only one moment in time. It says nothing about your growth. A nervous rider might even win a class but lose confidence doing it if fear controlled most of the ride.

Success for a sensitive or anxious rider can look like starting with a calm routine and breathing through mistakes. To adjusting the pace without panicking. Staying curious instead of being tense, and to finish the ride before fear takes over

If you did any of these, you succeeded. Real progress is emotional strength, not a placing.

Small Wins That Build Bravery

Bravery does not come from dramatic breakthroughs. It is created through many gentle moments of facing discomfort without forcing yourself.

A small win could be to trot one extra stride after taking a breath, to canter five seconds longer than yesterday or to walk past something spooky with curiosity instead of fear. Only ask for one transition instead of ten

These small wins add up. Over time, they turn into confidence that feels real.

Monthly Confidence Check

At the end of each month, focus on courage instead of results. Ask yourself:

1 When did I stay calm during something hard

2 When did I stop before fear overwhelmed me

3 What challenge did I face, even in a small way

4 Which skill feels a little easier now

Confidence grows slowly and with patience. These monthly reflections show you that progress is happening, even on days when your feelings make it hard to see.

Chapter 15

The Confident Rider Lifestyle

Riding confidence does not start the moment you sit in the saddle. It begins long before that, in the way you look after your body and your mind each day. A calm and confident lifestyle gives your nervous system something steady to stand on. It is tough to feel relaxed on a horse when your daily habits drain your energy and leave you tense.

Sleep and hydration affect your nerves

Lack of sleep does more than make you feel worn out. It increases stress and makes your body react more strongly to fear. Hydration matters just as much. When you do not drink enough water your muscles become less stable and your hands or legs may shake. Riders often think this shaky feeling means they are afraid, when it is really their body asking for support.

Before blaming yourself or your confidence, ask:

> Did I sleep enough this week
> Did I drink enough water today
> Am I physically prepared to ride

Basic self care lowers anxiety. Your body wants to help you feel steady and brave. You just need to give it what it needs.

Fitness without pressure

Fitness for riders is not about building bigger muscles or pushing through hard workouts. It is about stability, breath control, and smooth movement. Helpful exercises include: slow core engagement, balanced walking on varied surfaces, gentle hip mobility work, simple coordination drills and light stamina building

You do not have to train intensely. The goal is control instead of force. When your body feels steady, your brain feels safe.

The barn community affects confidence too

The environment where you ride can shape your confidence more than the horse does. A supportive barn is built on kindness, respect, and encouragement. A negative barn is built on gossip, judgment, and unhelpful competition.

A healthy barn community celebrates each riders progress, even the small wins. They will not use shame as a teaching tool and shares knowledge openly. Every rider's goals and comfort level will be respected.

If your barn makes you feel small, the problem is not you. The environment is failing you.

Build a circle that supports growth

Confidence grows when you are surrounded by people who help you feel safe. Choose a circle that:

Encourages steady progress, listens with respect, values effort more than perfection, helps you make calm choices and supports your personal boundaries.

No rider becomes brave alone. Confidence grows in a place where your body is cared for, your skills are respected, and your emotions are safe. When your world supports you, your riding will reflect it.

Part 6
Practical Workbooks

Chapter 16
Rider Training Worksheets

These workbook pages transform the ideas from this book into daily tools. They make progress visible and help you build confidence with structure. Every page is created with the ease of scanning or copying in mind.

Mindful Rein Studio

Confidence Score Sheet

Use this sheet once a week to track emotional progress. Never score yourself on performance or perfection. Score only on how calm, deliberate, and present you felt.

Confidence Score Sheet

Use this sheet once a week to track emotional progress. Never score yourself on performance or perfection. Score only on how calm, deliberate, and present you felt.

Criteria	1	2	3	Notes
I used slow breathing before mounting	☐	☐	☐	
I stayed curious when something felt hard	☐	☐	☐	
I communicated clearly with my instructor	☐	☐	☐	
I rode without judging myself	☐	☐	☐	
I ended the ride calmly	☐	☐	☐	
I noticed at least one thing that worked	☐	☐	☐	

Scoring Guide

One: I struggled with this
Two: I did it sometimes
Three: I did it well and calmly

At the bottom of the sheet, write:

My Calm Win of the Week: _____
Something I Learned About Myself: _____

Fear Ladder Template

Choose one situation that triggers fear. Break it into small steps. Each step should feel slightly uncomfortable, not overwhelming.

Fear Focus Goal: _____

Step	Action	How Did It Feel	Try Again or Move On
1			☐ Try again ☐ Move on
2			☐ Try again ☐ Move on
3			☐ Try again ☐ Move on
4			☐ Try again ☐ Move on
5			☐ Try again ☐ Move on

Notes for Next Ride: _____
Progress Reward: _____

Reward is not food or spending. It can be a break, a stretch, a moment to celebrate, or a kind message to yourself.

Mindful Rein Studio

Post Lesson Reflection Page

Use this after every lesson. Keep it simple and judgment free.

Date: _____
Horse: _____
Instructor: _____

Three things that went well:

One thing to improve without pressure:

What helped me stay calm today:

What I want to remember next time:

Optional calming rating:
- ☐ I felt unsafe
- ☐ I felt nervous
- ☐ I felt challenged
- ☐ I felt capable
- ☐ I felt confident

All of these are acceptable states, not success levels.

Monthly Bravery Challenges

Bravery is a habit. Choose one small challenge each week. It should take less than ten minutes.

Month: _____

Week	Challenge	Result	Feeling
1	_____	☐ Yes ☐ Not yet	☺ ☺ ☺
2	_____	☐ Yes ☐ Not yet	☺ ☺ ☺
3	_____	☐ Yes ☐ Not yet	☺ ☺ ☺
4	_____	☐ Yes ☐ Not yet	☺ ☺ ☺

At the end of the month:

What brave thing did I do most consistently:

What surprised me in a good way:

Next month's confidence focus:

Mindful Rein Studio

Calm Routine Checklist

Use this before every ride. Tick each step slowly, not quickly.

Calm Routine Checklist

Use this before every ride. Tick each step slowly, not quickly.

- ☐ Breathe out with long exhale
- ☐ Relax jaw and lips
- ☐ Drop shoulders
- ☐ Release grip in thighs
- ☐ Soften reins between fingers
- ☐ Mount with one calm breath
- ☐ Start in walk with rhythm breathing
- ☐ Set one simple intention for this ride
- ☐ End before fear grows

My intention today: _____

Show Diary Workbook

A diary for show days, clinics, or first attempts at new challenges. Focus on presence, not scores.

Event: _____
Horse: _____
Goal for this day: _____

Warm Up Notes
What helped: _____
What I changed: _____

During My Ride
I remembered to:
☐ Breathe
☐ Stay curious
☐ Fix one thing only
☐ Reward effort
☐ Smile for my horse

After the Ride
What worked well: _____
How I handled mistakes: _____
What my horse taught me today: _____

A moment I am proud of: _____

Optional: attach photos, numbers, or ribbons only if they add joy.

Daily Mindset Affirmations

Choose one per day. Repeat it while grooming, mounting, or breathing.

Daily Mindset Affirmations

Choose one per day. Repeat it while grooming, mounting, or breathing.

- ☐ I train calmness, not perfection.
- ☐ My breath steadies my horse.
- ☐ Every step is progress, even slow ones.
- ☐ I ride with curiosity instead of fear.
- ☐ Small wins build great confidence.
- ☐ My horse feels safe when I slow down.
- ☐ I am allowed to take my time.
- ☐ I am learning, not performing.
- ☐ Calm riding is strong riding.
- ☐ I choose steady progress today.

Space for your own affirmation:

Letter to Your Future Confident Self

Write this as if you already achieved what you are working toward. Describe how you feel, how you ride, and how you care for your horse.

Write freely, without rules:

Afterword: Confidence Is a Skill You Build, Not a Personality Trait

You may have heard people say that some riders are born confident. You may have believed that courage is a personality you either have or do not have. Look back through the pages you have just completed and notice something important. At no point were you asked to be fearless. You were asked to breathe, to observe, to take one small step, and then another. None of this depends on being a brave person. It depends on building a brave habit.

Confidence is not a gift. It is a practice.

If you are a rider who feels nervous, that does not mean you are less capable. It means you are human. It means your body and mind have been trying to protect you. Fear is not your enemy. It is a message asking for guidance. When you listen to it with care instead of force, you learn how to ride with clarity rather than panic.

You have now gathered tools that help you reset, refocus, and rebuild trust one moment at a time. You have learned how

Afterword: Confidence Is a Skill You Build, Not a Personality Trait

breath can steady your hands, how curiosity can soften mistakes, and how small wins can grow into strong foundations. You have seen that fear can change a ride, but so can a calm exhale, a thoughtful choice, or a gentle boundary. You have not conquered fear. You have begun to train it.

Remember this: growth is quiet. It appears in small adjustments, tiny improvements, and choices others may never see. You will not always recognise your progress right away, but it is happening each time you pause instead of panic, observe instead of judge, and continue instead of give up.

Confidence is not loud. It does not rush. It does not force. It grows slowly, like trust between horse and rider. You build it with patience, repetition, and kindness toward yourself. You do not need big jumps, high speeds, or perfect rounds to prove strength. You only need the willingness to keep practicing with respect for your own pace.

If fear arrives again, do not assume you have gone backward. It simply means you have reached a new layer to train. You already know how to approach it. You already know how to breathe, how to step back, how to break a challenge into pieces. The difference now is that you have a path instead of uncertainty.

Your horse does not need you to be fearless. Your horse needs you to be aware, present, and willing to learn. Confidence will follow. It will show up in the way you handle setbacks, the way you choose curiosity, and the way you offer yourself another chance.

Afterword: Confidence Is a Skill You Build, Not a Personality Trait

Keep practicing. Some days will feel strong, and others not so much, but both will teach you. You are not trying to become a rider without fear. You are becoming a rider who knows how to guide it.

> That is confidence.

And you are building it, one calm breath at a time.

The Voice Behind this Book

This book was written by Annalie, a lifelong horsewoman who has spent decades riding, retraining, and breeding horses. Her early years with off-track Thoroughbreds, guiding them from the tension of racing into the balance and focus needed for showjumping, shaped her belief that horses become confident when riders learn to listen with patience rather than pressure. Through Mindful Rein Studio, she now shares quiet, practical tools that help riders train the mind behind the reins. These pages are offered not as instruction from above, but as guidance from a fellow rider who has learned, and continues to learn, alongside every horse.

www.ingramcontent.com/pod-product-compliance
Lightning Source LLC
Chambersburg PA
CBHW052112070526
44584CB00017B/2455